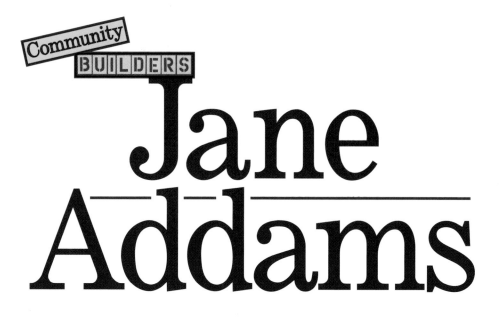

Community BUILDERS

Jane Addams

Community BUILDERS

Jane Addams

Pioneer Social Worker

by Charnan Simon

Children's Press®
A Division of Grolier Publishing
New York London Hong Kong Sydney
Danbury, Connecticut

Photo Credits

Photographs ©: AP/Wide World Photos: 9, 16; Archive Photos: cover; Brown Brothers: 14, 21; Chicago Historical Society: 18; Corbis-Bettmann: 7, 12, 13, 31, 34, 37; Culver Pictures: 32; FW file: 22; Impact Visuals: 44 (Carolina Kroon); New York Public Library Picture Collection: 8, 23; Photo Researchers: 45 (Jeff Greenberg); Underwood & Underwood/Corbis-Bettmann: 3, 25 bottom, 35; University of Illinois at Chicago, The University Library: 11, 25 top, 33, 40 (Jane Addams Memorial Collection), 17, 39, 42 (Jane Addams Memorial Collection, Wallace Kirkland Papers) back cover, 43 (University Archives); UPI/Corbis-Bettmann: 2, 26, 27, 29, 30, 38.

Author photograph ©: Tom Kazunas

Library of Congress Cataloging-in-Publication Data

Simon, Charnan.
    Jane Addams : pioneer social worker / by Charnan Simon.
       p. cm. — (Community builders)
    Includes bibliographical references and index.
    Summary: Presents the life of the woman whose devotion to social work led to her establishing Hull House in Chicago and who was awarded the Nobel Peace Prize in 1931.
    ISBN: 0-516-20391-6 (lib. bdg.)   0-516-26235-1 (pbk.)
    1. Addams, Jane, 1860-1935—Juvenile literature. 2. Women social workers—United States—Biography—Juvenile literature. 3. Women social reformers—United States—Biography—Juvenile literature. [1. Addams, Jane, 1860–1935. 2. Social workers. 3. Reformers. 4. Women—Biography.] I. Title. II. Series: Simon, Charnan. Community builders.
HV40.32.A33S55 1997
361.3'092—dc21
[B]   96-54042
                                                CIP
                                                AC

Contents

Chapter ONE

Imagine This: Then and Now

Imagine that it is morning at your house. You and your family are getting ready for school and work. You are helping your little brother decide what to take to kindergarten for show-and-tell. Your dad is dressing your little sister for her day-care center. Your mom is getting breakfast ready: cereal, or pancakes, or bagels and cream cheese. The telephone rings, and it's your best friend asking if you'll meet her at the playground.

6

**Immigrants to America often arrived
with few possessions and little money.**

Now imagine that you live one hundred years
ago. You and your family have just come to the
United States from across the Atlantic Ocean. You
are so poor that there is never enough food for a

During the late 1800s, most children were expected
to work in factories instead of going to school.

healthy breakfast. Your mom and dad both have to work—and so do you. Even though you are only eight years old, you are old enough to earn money for your family. Instead of attending school, you work in a noisy, dangerous factory all day long. There is no kindergarten for your brother and no day-care center for your sister, so they have to stay home by themselves. None of you has time to play, and even if you did, there are no public playgrounds.

This is what life was like for many families in American cities one hundred years ago. A woman named Jane Addams didn't think it was fair. She worked all of her life to make life better for children and their families. This is the story of how she did it.

Jane Addams

Chapter TWO

A Happy Childhood

Jane Addams was born on September 6, 1860, in the little town of Cedarville, Illinois. Even though Jane's mother died when she was just two years old, Jane had a happy childhood. She lived in a big, comfortable house. Her four older sisters and brothers pampered her and played with her. Jane adored her father. Later there would be a stepmother to care for Jane, too.

The Civil War was raging in the United States during Jane's childhood. Southern states were fighting for their way of life, which included owning

10

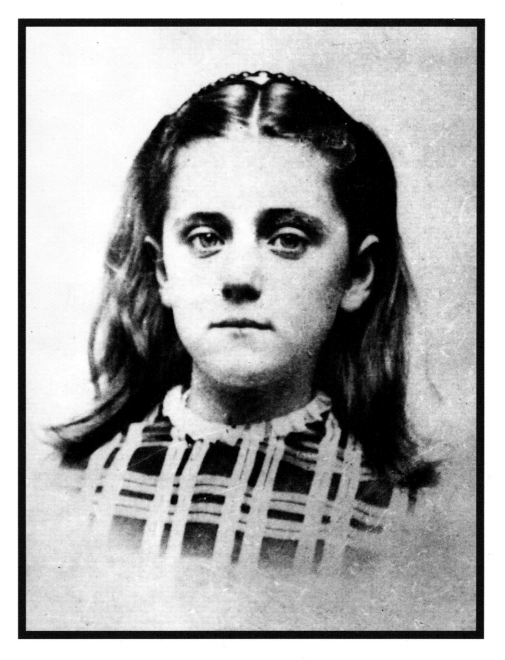

Growing up in Illinois, Jane enjoyed many privileges that other children didn't have.

black slaves. Northern states were fighting to stop slavery and to keep the country together.

Jane's father, John Addams, did not believe in slavery. He didn't think it was right for one human being to own another human being. As a Quaker, John Addams wouldn't fight in the war. But he supported the Northern states and was a good friend of President Abraham Lincoln. For Jane's entire life, she would remember how she felt on the sad day when President Lincoln was killed. She was only four years old at the time, and it was the first time she had ever seen grown-ups cry.

Abraham Lincoln died on April 14, 1865, just a few days after the end of the Civil War.

Jane learned many important lessons from her father and his Quaker beliefs. She learned to think carefully about right and wrong. She learned to listen to other peo-

The Quakers

Quakers are members of the Religious Society of Friends, a branch of Christianity. Quakers are pacifists, which means that they don't believe in war or fighting. Instead, they try to solve problems peacefully. Quakers think education is very important. They like to learn all they can about a problem, and then solve it to make the world a better place to live.

A Quaker church in the 1800s

ple and to respect their ideas and beliefs. Jane also learned to trust her own feelings, and to work hard to change things that were not fair.

Jane Addams felt sorry for children who had to play
in city streets because there were no playgrounds.

Chapter THREE

Jane's Big Idea

Even though Jane Addams had a safe and happy childhood, she knew that not everyone was so lucky. Some children were cold and hungry. They lived in poorhouses and worked long hours in big factories. Jane didn't think this was right. She vowed that when she grew up, she would own a big house where poor children could come and play whenever they wanted.

Jane Addams did what she promised, but it wasn't easy. When Jane was just twenty years old, her father died. A few months later, she had a dangerous operation on her back. For a long time after her surgery, Jane was tired and unhappy. After she graduated from college, she wanted to do something useful with her life. But she did not know what that something should be.

Then, when Jane was twenty-seven years old, she went to Europe with her good friend, Ellen Gates Starr. The

Jane at age twenty-one, when she graduated from college

two young women visited a place called Toynbee Hall in London, England. Toynbee Hall was a settlement house located in a run-down neighborhood in London. It was called a "settlement house" because men from a nearby university came there to settle in the neighborhood and work among poor people. The university men wanted to help the neighbors around Toynbee Hall live a better life. At the same time, they wanted to learn from their working-class neighbors. They hoped that by studying what made people poor, they could learn how to stop poverty forever.

Ellen Gates Starr assisted Jane in her efforts to establish a settlement house in the United States.

Seeing all the good work being done at Toynbee Hall gave Jane Addams her big idea. Jane's father had left her a great deal of money when he died. She decided to use that money to start her own settlement house in the United States—in Chicago, Illinois. Jane wanted her house to be located in one of the poorest parts of Chicago.

17

From this house, Jane would help anyone in the neighborhood who needed her. At last she would make her childhood dream of helping the poor come true.

Jane wanted her settlement house to be located in a poor immigrant neighborhood such as this one.

Chicago, Illinois

Chicago, Illinois, is located in the midwestern United States, along the shores of Lake Michigan. It was founded as a city in 1837, but American Indians had lived in the area for more than five thousand years. When Jane Addams bought her house in 1889, more than one million people lived in the city. Today, about three million people call Chicago home.

Chapter FOUR

Pioneer Social Worker

O nce Jane Addams made up her mind to do something, there was no stopping her. With her friend Ellen at her side, she soon found just the right house.

The house sat in the middle of a crowded immigrant neighborhood. Many of Jane's neighbors had just come to the United States from European countries. Like other recent immigrants in the United States, they were not always treated fairly. They couldn't speak English, and their customs were different.

This building was abandoned until Jane turned it
into a settlement house for the community.

Immigrants

An immigrant is a person who leaves one country to live permanently in another. In the early 1900s, millions of people immigrated to the United States from Europe.

Many immigrants could barely afford to live in one-room apartments.

Many of the families in the area lived in run-down houses. They could not afford warm clothing or enough food. Some didn't even have clean water to drink. The neighborhood children had no place to play. Their mothers and fathers worked in factories all day long. Sometimes the children worked, too. Sometimes they had to stay home alone while their parents worked.

22

Child Labor

For hundreds of years in the United States, young children worked in factories, mines, or on farms. Some of these workers were only seven years old. They didn't earn much money, even though they worked for many hours each day. Childrens' work was usually dangerous. Most child workers were not healthy because of poor working conditions. For many years, people such as Jane Addams worked hard to end child labor.

These young boys worked in a coal mine.

Jane decided to call her house Hull House. When she and Ellen moved in on September 18, 1889, it was the beginning of a great American experiment.

A neighborhood center such as Hull House was a brand-new idea in the United States in 1889. There was nobody to tell Jane what to do or how to do it, so she made things up as she went along. But at all times, she tried to provide whatever her community needed.

Hungry children and working people could always receive a bowl of soup and a glass of milk at Hull House. Immigrants could take English lessons. Young working women could rent clean, safe, inexpensive rooms in which to live.

Jane saw how hard it was for mothers to find safe places to leave their children while they went to work. So she started Chicago's first day-care center in a cottage near Hull House. Within a few years, she had also opened a kindergarten. Next she built a playground where any child could play. It was the first public playground in the United States.

It was hard work for Jane to run Hull House, but she always found time to read or play with the children.

Hull House provided children with safe places to play and learn.

Children at Hull House had many activities to choose from. These children are learning to make pottery.

Jane Addams wanted her immigrant neighbors to feel at home in their new country. She also wanted them to remember the customs and culture of their homelands. She encouraged them to share their native literature, art, music, and cooking with each other. On some nights, Hull House rang with German songs and poetry. Other nights were devoted to Irish dancing or Italian cooking. Jane made sure that everyone at Hull House had something to share.

Jane and Ellen kept thinking of new things to do at Hull House. They put on plays and held debates. They offered college classes. They taught art, music, and crafts. They opened a gym where young people could exercise and play games. They made Hull House a true community center where everyone was welcome, and everyone was equal.

Word of what Jane Addams was doing at Hull House spread. Young men and women from all over the country came to work with Jane. They wanted to learn how to help the poor neighborhoods in their own cities. Hull House became a teaching center for social workers everywhere.

Hull House became a training ground for future social workers (such as the adults in this photo).

Jane welcomed these young men and women. She had always wanted Hull House to serve two purposes. Of course, she wanted it to help the poor people who lived in the neighborhood. But Jane also wanted Hull House to help more fortunate young people find a worthy occupation. Jane remembered how awful she had felt after she graduated from college, not knowing what to do with her life. Now she welcomed the chance to show other educated young

Who Are Social Workers?

Social workers try to help people solve problems caused by poverty, crime, illness, unemployment, and homelessness. Social work became a profession in the late 1800s, at about the same time that Jane Addams was opening Hull House.

Hull House encouraged people throughout the neighborhood to help each other. While walking past Hull House, this man stopped to help a little girl who wasn't tall enough to reach the water fountain.

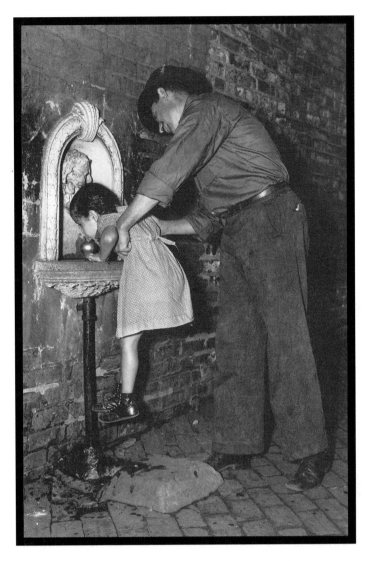

people how to put their talents and energies to use serving others. Many remarkable men and women came to work with Jane Addams at Hull House. Together, they worked to change their Chicago community to make it a better place to live.

Chapter FIVE

Beyond Hull House

Jane Addams knew that her work at Hull House was important. But her Chicago neighborhood was just a small part of the large United States. Jane wanted to make life better for people everywhere.

Jane worked hard to change the laws of the country in order to make factory owners treat their workers

Jane (third from right) became active in organizations that tried to improve life for the country's workers.

better. She fought in favor of higher wages, shorter working hours, and a cleaner, safer environment for workers.

Jane also worked to make life easier for children. She fought for laws that would take children out of unsafe factories and put them in classrooms where they could learn. And she was one of the first people in

Jane believed that children deserved to be learning in schools, instead of working in factories.

the United States to see how important it was to have public playgrounds where even the poorest children could play in the fresh air.

Jane Addams also fought for women's rights. In those days, most people believed that women belonged in the home. But Jane believed that women should be allowed to study and to

31

Jane (right) worked hard in support of women's right to vote.

work the same way men did. She also thought that women should be allowed to vote. She worked hard to change the laws in the United States so that women could vote.

The Nineteenth Amendment

Imagine that in your classroom, only boys could vote on what to play at recess or which book to read at storytime. Would that be fair? When Jane Addams was young, only men could vote. In 1920, the Nineteenth Amendment to the U.S. Constitution was passed. It gave all women in the United States the right to vote.

**Hull House appeared on the cover
of *Twenty Years at Hull House*.**

When Jane wasn't at Hull House in Chicago, she traveled tirelessly, sharing her ideas on changing society. She wrote thousands of letters asking wealthy people to contribute money to Hull House and to her other projects. She even found time to write books. The story about her life as an activist and social worker, *Twenty Years at Hull House,* became a best-seller as soon as it was published in 1910.

One of Jane Addams's greatest challenges came when World War I started in 1914. Jane still shared the Quaker belief in pacifism. She insisted

World War I

World War I started in Europe on June 28, 1914. Within a few weeks, almost all of the countries in Europe were fighting. The United States entered the war in 1917.

World War I ended in 1918. During its four years, more than ten million people were killed. Many of them died in the fighting. Others died from disease or starvation.

A ship full of U.S. soldiers sets sail for Europe during World War I.

Jane (fourth from left) helped to start the Woman's Peace Party, which spoke out against war.

that no good could ever come out of violence or fighting. She believed that people must talk to each other in order to solve their problems peacefully.

Jane Addams spoke out strongly against the war. In 1915, she helped to start the Woman's Peace Party in the United States. Later that year she traveled to Europe to organize an international women's peace movement. Jane's work at Hull House had convinced her that people of all races and nationalities could get along peacefully. The world was, after all, one big community of neighbors.

Not everyone agreed with Jane. When the United States entered the war in 1917, many people called Jane a coward and a traitor. A traitor is a person who betrays, or turns against, his or her country. They said that if she really loved her country, she would support its war efforts. Even some of her closest friends turned against her.

Jane was sorry that many people disagreed with her, but she was determined to follow her own beliefs. She supported the war effort in her own way. Jane helped to provide food for the millions of hungry Europeans who didn't have enough to eat because of the fighting.

After the war, Jane traveled to Europe. She was horrified at how many starving people she found. Jane worked even harder to send food to all the war-torn countries. She didn't care whether the food went to people from the countries that fought against the United States.

Once again many Americans were angry with Jane. They didn't understand why she would help people who had just been enemies of the United

36

World War I left much of Europe in ruins.

States. But Jane believed that the best way to turn
an enemy into a friend was to lend a helping hand.
Patiently, she explained again and again: We are all
neighbors. The world is our community.

Before the war, one magazine article had called Jane Addams "the only saint America has produced." After the war, another article said she was "the most dangerous woman in America."

It was a hard time for Jane Addams, but she continued to speak out on issues that mattered to her. She also helped to form the American Civil Liberties Union (ACLU). The ACLU was dedicated to protecting people's right to speak out, even about unpopular subjects.

Although Jane was criticized in the United States, she was admired by people in other countries. In 1919,

After World War I, Jane traveled throughout Europe to share her views on peace.

she traveled to The Hague, Netherlands. While she was there, she helped to organize the Women's International League for Peace and Freedom (WIL).

At the fortieth anniversary of Hull House, Jane (seated, center) celebrated with friends and fellow Hull House workers.

As president of the WIL, Jane spent the next fifteen years traveling around the world to encourage cooperation among nations.

Gradually, people in the United States once again began to praise and to admire Jane. They grew to respect her pacifist views. When Hull House celebrated its fortieth birthday in 1929, hundreds of people came to honor Jane for her good works. Jane published *The Second Twenty Years at Hull House,* in 1930. In 1931, she received her greatest honor of all—the Nobel Peace Prize.

Jane Addams donated her Nobel Prize money to the Women's International League. She also gave the money she received from several other prizes to help the unemployed people in the neighborhood around Hull House. Although she had traveled far from her Chicago home, Hull House was always first in her heart.

The Nobel Prize bears the image of Alfred Nobel, its founder.

The Nobel Prizes

Nobel Prizes are the most honored prizes in the world. They were established by Alfred Nobel, the Swedish engineer who invented dynamite. In his will, Nobel instructed that all of his money should be used to fund yearly prizes for people who have made valuable contributions to the "good of humanity." The first Nobel Prizes were awarded in 1901.

Chapter SIX
After Hull House

Jane Addams never stopped wanting to make the world a better place. When she died at the age of seventy-four on May 21, 1935, thousands of men, women, and children went to her funeral. Hull House neighbors mingled with international leaders as they all gathered to pay tribute to a great American woman.

Perhaps Jane summed up her own life best in one of her final speeches: "Nothing could be worse than the fear that one had given up too soon, and had left one effort unexpended which might have saved the world."

People from all over the world gathered in the Hull House courtyard to pay their respects to Jane following her death in 1935.

The work at Hull House continued long after Jane Addams died. By the 1960s, the Hull House Association had spread from the original settlement house to more than forty locations around Chicago. Today, Hull House workers still offer hope and help to Chicago's neediest families.

The neighborhood around Hull House looks different now from the way it looked when Jane lived there. Most of the old buildings have been torn down to make room for the Chicago campus of the University of Illinois.

But the original house that Jane Addams and Ellen Gates Starr moved into in 1889 is still standing. It has been preserved as a museum and it looks just like it did when Jane lived there. Every year thousands of visitors pass through its doors to look at the newspaper clippings, photographs, and films that tell the story of Hull House—and Jane Addams.

Today, Hull House is a museum where visitors can learn more about Jane Addams and her social work.

In Your Community

Jane Addams wanted to make everyone's community a good place to live. She opened Hull House to give the poor people of Chicago a place to go when they needed help.

Does your town have a community center? Have you ever taken part in any of its activities? Sometimes community centers include swimming pools, basketball courts, and playgrounds. Sometimes they have food pantries or offer counseling services.

Find out what kinds of activities and assistance are offered at your community center.

Timeline

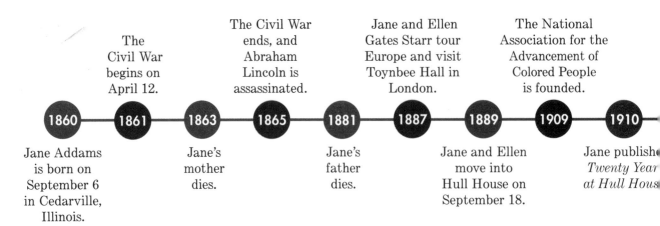

The Civil War begins on April 12.

The Civil War ends, and Abraham Lincoln is assassinated.

Jane and Ellen Gates Starr tour Europe and visit Toynbee Hall in London.

The National Association for the Advancement of Colored People is founded.

1860 — **1861** — **1863** — **1865** — **1881** — **1887** — **1889** — **1909** — **1910**

Jane Addams is born on September 6 in Cedarville, Illinois.

Jane's mother dies.

Jane's father dies.

Jane and Ellen move into Hull House on September 18.

Jane publishe
Twenty Year
at Hull Hous

• Does your community center hold food drives or clothing drives? Ask a parent or teacher how you can help donate to the drive.

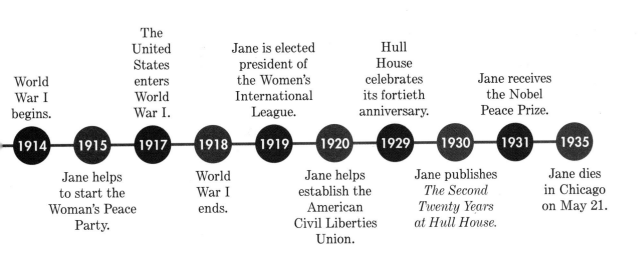

• Are there activities for younger children such as games or storytime? Perhaps you can spend time reading to the children.

• Do elderly people from your community gather at the center for arts and crafts, card games, or sing-alongs? Maybe you can assist them by passing out materials and helping with cutting or pasting.

If your town doesn't have a community center, there are still many things you can do to help your community. Perhaps you can organize a neighborhood clean-up with other students from your class. Or invite children from a school that doesn't have a playground to play at your school's playground. What other activities can you think of? Whatever ideas you have, be sure to ask an adult for help and supervision.

World War I begins.
1914

Jane helps to start the Woman's Peace Party.
1915

The United States enters World War I.
1917

World War I ends.
1918

Jane is elected president of the Women's International League.
1919

Jane helps establish the American Civil Liberties Union.
1920

Hull House celebrates its fortieth anniversary.
1929

Jane publishes *The Second Twenty Years at Hull House.*
1930

Jane receives the Nobel Peace Prize.
1931

Jane dies in Chicago on May 21.
1935

To Find Out More

Here are some additional resources to help you learn more about Jane Addams, Hull House, and groups that are carrying on Jane's work:

Books

Addams, Jane. *Twenty Years at Hull House.* University of Illinois Press, 1990.

Kent, Deborah. *Jane Addams and Hull House.* Children's Press, 1992.

Kittredge, Mary. *Jane Addams: A Centennial Reader.* Chelsea House Publishers, 1988.

McPherson, Stephanie Sammartino. *Peace and Bread: The Story of Jane Addams.* Carolrhoda Books, Inc., 1993.

Mitchard, Jacquelyn. *Jane Addams: Pioneer in Social Reform and Activist for World Peace.* Gareth Stevens Children's Books, 1991.

Organizations and Online Sites

Hull House Youth Advocate Program
6042 South Indiana
Chicago, IL 60637

Jane Addams — Hull House Association
10 South Riverside Plaza
Suite 1720
Chicago, IL 60606
http://www.terasys.com/hullhouse/

Jane Addams — Hull House Museum
800 South Halstead
Chicago, IL 60607
http://cpl.lib.uic.edu/004chicago/ timeline/hullhouse.html

The Peace Museum
350 West Ontario Street
Chicago, IL 60610

Index

About the Author

Charnan Simon lives in Madison, Wisconsin, with her husband and her two daughters. She is a former editor at *Cricket* magazine, and sometimes works at a children's bookstore called Pooh Corner. But mainly she likes reading and writing books and spending time with her family.

Ms. Simon lived in Chicago, Illinois, for many years. She often walked past the Hull House Museum on the corner of Halsted and Polk Streets. Learning about Jane Addams's life has been a tremendously rewarding experience for the author.